God's Love Story:
The Story of God's Love from Before the Beginning
Book 2

By R. Lane Lender

STORIES OF LIFE PRODUCTIONS

God's Love Story: The Story of God's Love from Before the Beginning, Book 2

Copyright © 2020 By Stories of Life Productions

ISBN: 978-1-970032-03-1 (Hard Cover)

ISBN: 978-1-970032-05-5 (eBook)

For more information about Stories of Life Productions and/or God's Love Story Visual Bible visit www.glsvb.org.

All rights reserved. No part of this publication may be reproduced, stored in a retrieval system, or transmitted in any form or by any means – electronic, mechanical, photocopy, recording, or any other – except for brief quotations in printed reviews, without the prior permission of Stories of Life Productions.

Published in the United States of America

Introduction

God's Love Story Children's Book Series is dedicated to my grandchildren. One of the greatest gifts a parent can pass off to their children is a passion to love Jesus more than anything else in this world. This passion is more caught than taught. Our children need to see our love for Jesus and they too will follow in our footsteps. My wife and I are truly blessed to not only have godly parents but to have two wonderful children, now in their mid twenties, who have learned to love Jesus from birth. As I write, my son is a prosecuting attorney in Texas and my daughter is married to a wonderful man, a dedicated Christ follower. They now have one child and their hope is many more. My daughter is also preparing to homeschool them all like she and her brother were. My desire is to provide a biblically-based tool for parents to use to cultivate in their children a love for Jesus in their most precious and formative years. I desire nothing more than to see my future grandchildren come to know Jesus and to develop into solid Kingdom contributing Christ followers. Thus, I submit this contribution. My prayer is that this book series develops in your children a love for the gospel and a passion for Jesus.

I also want to thank you for your purchase of this book and the other books in this series (See the back cover for more details). Your purchase goes directly to support Stories of Life Productions as we continue to produce, promote, and distribute God's Love Story Visual Bible (GLSVB). GLSVB is an oral story Bible created for the cell phone that has been translated into several languages of Unreached People Groups (UPGs). These UPGs live in places that are very difficult to access with the gospel. Because of your purchase, as well as gifts from generous donors, GLSVB is provided free to missionaries and believers around the world who are using this tool for evangelism and discipleship. GLSVB can be accessed at www.hikayaat.com. To find out more information, order books, or help us promote God's Love Story Children's Book series or GLSVB, visit www.glsvb.org. May God's Love Story Children's Books give you and your child a passion to serve Christ and His Kingdom's purpose!

Sincerely,
R. Lane Lender
Stories of Life Productions
contact@glsvb.org
www.hikayaat.com
www.glsvb.org

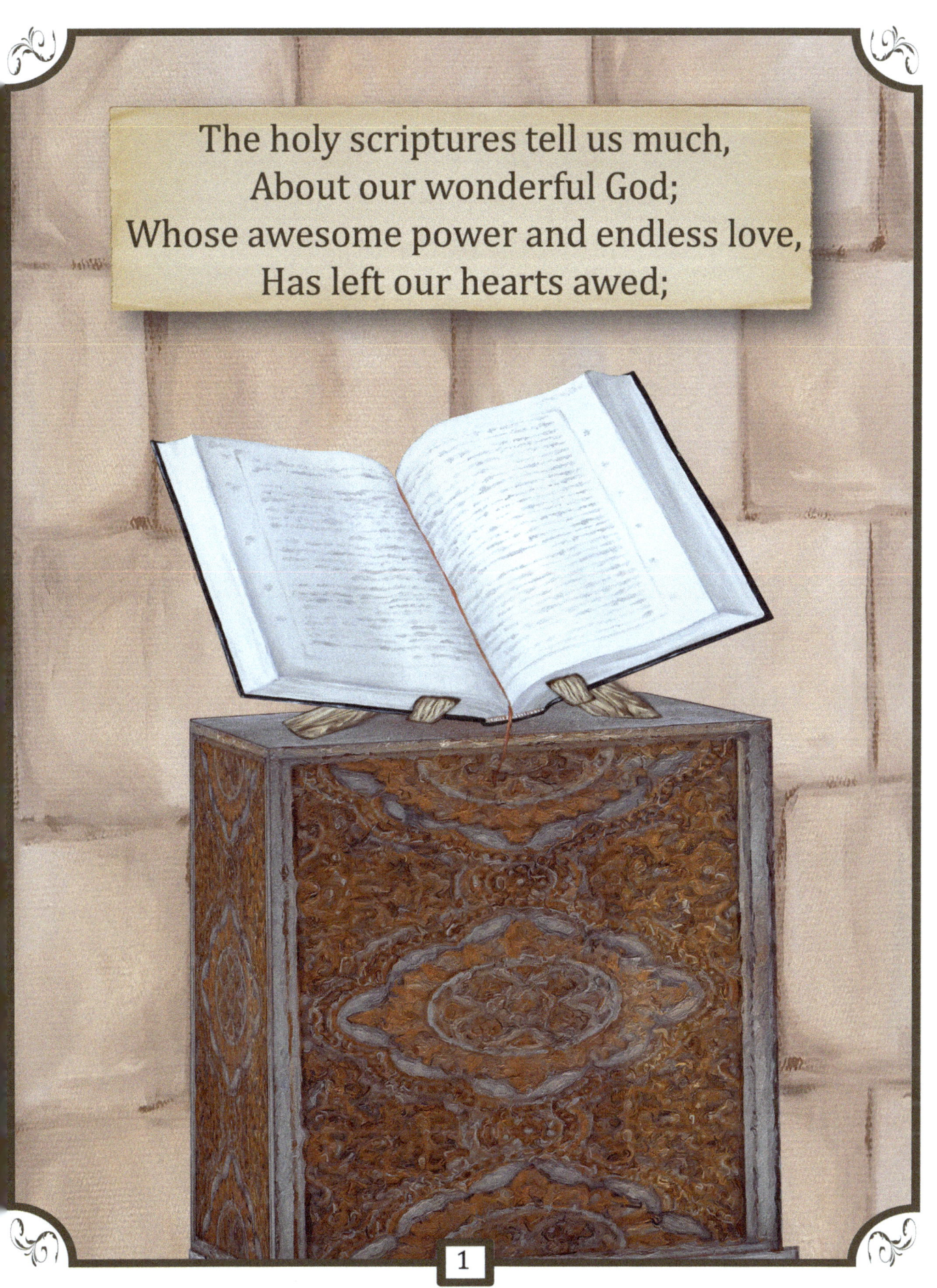

The holy scriptures tell us much,
About our wonderful God;
Whose awesome power and endless love,
Has left our hearts awed;

With careful hands and perfect knowledge,
God fashioned all the world;
He set the moon and hung the stars,
The universe unfurled;

The sky, the earth, the grass, the trees,
Were made by the Almighty;
The animals with the breath of life,
So perfect and so tidy;

But before God made all there is,
He created many angels;
The angels are His messengers,
To serve Him through the ages;

He created so many angels,
That none could ever count;
They served His purpose far and wide,
As He called them to account;

The greatest angel of them all,
How beautiful was he;
Glowing white a brilliant sight,
It was Lucifer you see;

So he convinced a third of them,
To turn their backs on God;
In little time their fate was sealed,
On God's truth they trod;

Their sin God would not tolerate,
Nor would He their rebellion;
Away from Him He cast them out,
The cost of their transgression;

To and fro they walked the earth,
Seeking to devour;
Anyone they can convince,
Our hearts they want to sour;

To yield to Satan's plan on earth,
To follow to destruction;
Wide is the path that leads to death,
Eternal life's obstruction;

But Jesus came to conquer death,
And give us victory;
Through our Lord there is no fear,
Overcoming the enemy;

By the blood of the Lamb,
We will overcome;
By the word of our testimony,
We are not undone;

So stand with Christ and you will see,
There's nothing er' to fear;
Jesus is our conquering King,
So let us all draw near;

Lightning Source UK Ltd.
Milton Keynes UK
UKHW050833110820
367866UK00008B/116

9 781970 032031